EX LIBRIS

Great Creatures of the World
BIG CATS

Facts On File

Big Cats
A Great Creatures of the World book

Written by Susan Lumpkin

Facts On File, Inc.
460 Park Avenue South
New York NY 10016

Copyright © 1993 Weldon Owen Pty Limited
Copyright © 1993 Weldon Owen Inc.

Produced by Weldon Owen Pty Limited
43 Victoria Street, McMahons Point,
NSW 2060, Australia
Telex AA23038, Fax (02)929 8352
A member of the Weldon International
Group of Companies
Sydney • London • San Francisco

Chairman: Kevin Weldon
President: John Owen
General Manager: Stuart Laurence
Publisher: Sheena Coupe
Project Coordinator: Tracy Tucker
Copy Editor: Beverley Barnes
Assistant Editor: Veronica Hilton
Designer: Diane Quick
Main Illustrations: Frank Knight
Other Illustrations: Tony Pyrzakowski
Production Director: Mick Bagnato
Production Coordinator: Simone Perryman
DTP Bureau: High Q Resolutions, Sydney

Printed by Kyodo Printing Co. (Singapore) Pty Ltd
Printed in Singapore

A WELDON OWEN PRODUCTION

10 9 8 7 6 5 4 3 2 1

About the author
Dr. Susan Lumpkin received her Ph.D. in biological psychology, specializing in animal behavior, at Duke University. She was awarded a Smithsonian Institution Post-doctoral Fellowship for advanced study in mammalian behavior at the National Zoological Park. Dr. Lumpkin has conducted extensive research in mammalian and avian reproductive behavior and has written widely on animal behavior and conservation for general audiences. She was coordinating editor of *Wild Mammals in Captivity: A Guide to Management*, co-consulting editor on *Great Cats*, and is editor of the Friends of the National Zoo *Zoogoer* magazine.

Facts On File books are available at special discounts when purchased in bulk quantities for businesses, associations, institutions or sales promotions. Please call our Special Sales Department in New York at 212/683-2244 (dial 800/322-8755 except in NY, AK or HI).

Library of Congress
Cataloging-in-Publication Data:

Lumpkin, Susan
    Big cats / [written by Susan Lumpkin]
    p. cm. — (Great Creatures of the World)
    Includes index.
    Summary: Describes the physical characteristics and behavior of the larger feline species in their habitats around the world.
    ISBN 0-8160-2847-8
    1. Felidae—Juvenile literature [1. Felidae. 2. Cats.]
    I. Title. II. Series
    QL 737.C23L86 1993   92-26838
    599.74'428—dc20   CIP AC

The author would like to acknowledge the following people whose contributions to *Great Cats* were drawn upon for this book:

Dr. Brian Bertram
Dr. John David Bygott
Dr. T.M. Caro
Mr. John A. Cavallo
Mr. Ravi Chellam
Dr. Louise H. Emmons
Dr. Jeannette Hanby
Dr. Fred P. Heald
Mr. Peter Jackson
Mr. Rodney Jackson
Dr. A.J.T. Johnsingh
Mr. K. Ullas Karanth
Dr. Richard A. Kiltie
Ms. M. Karen Laurenson
Dr. Charles McDougal
Mr. Jeffrey A. McNeely
Ms. Robin Meadows
Ms. Sriyanie Miththapala
Dr. Nancy A. Neff
Dr. Stephen J. O'Brien
Dr. Gustav Peters
Dr. John Seidensticker
Mr. Christopher A. Shaw
Dr. Jan Stuart
Ms. Fiona C. Sunquist
Dr. Mel Sunquist
Dr. Ronald L. Tilson
Dr. Blaire Van Valkenburgh
Ms. Lisa Florman Weinberg
Dr. David E. Wildt

Jonathan Scott/Planet Earth Pictures

Belinda Wright/DRK Photo

Mark Deeble & Victoria Stone

Page 1: Male lions often die in bloody battles over females.
Pages 2–3: A female African lion chases a herd of wildebeests from a waterhole.
This page (top to bottom):
A cheetah cub has a woolly "baby" coat until it is about four months of age.
A Bengal tiger on the lookout for prey.
Watchful female lions look over their territory.
Opposite page: Two cheetahs climb a candelabra tree in East Africa.
Page 6: Leopards can swim but are not often seen in water.
Page 7: (top) A male lion grimaces in response to a receptive female.
(bottom) A tiger cools down during the heat of a tropical day.

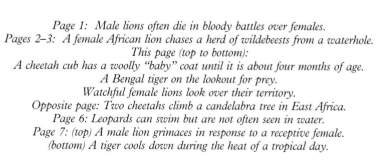

Contents

What are big cats?

From tabbies to tigers, all cats are powerful hunters with deadly sharp teeth, strong jaws, and agile bodies.

Most cats are small. In 30 species, or kinds, the adults weigh 44 pounds (20 kilograms) or less. The other seven species are called "big cats." Lions and tigers, the largest cats, have an average weight between 308 and 440 pounds (140–200 kilograms). Medium-sized jaguars, leopards, pumas, and snow leopards usually weigh between 88 and 176 pounds (40–80 kilograms). Cheetahs are slightly smaller. But all seven are rightly called big cats.

Just like people, individual cats can vary greatly in size. The largest jaguars or leopards may be bigger than the smallest tigers. In human terms, this range would be from the "90–pound weakling" of cartoons to the 300–pound giants who protect the quarterback in football!

Cats are mammals—warm-blooded, fur-covered animals that feed milk to their young. Cats belong to one particular group of mammals, the order Carnivora. This order includes the cat family (Felidae) and 10 other families of mammals that have features designed for a diet of meat. In fact, the words *Carnivora* and *carnivore* mean "meat-eater."

Different groupings

Size divides the cats into big and small; and size is very important to the way that cats live and find food. But scientists look at other features to form different groupings of cats. Five of the big cats belong to the same genus—a group of species more closely related to each other than to any other species. Lions, tigers, leopards, jaguars, and snow leopards belong to the genus *Panthera*.

Peter Johnson/NHPA

▲ *The long mane of a male lion makes it easy for us to tell male and female lions apart. Lions are the only cats with such obvious differences between males and females, but in all cats, the males are usually larger than the females.*

Claudia Wright/Partridge Productions/Oxford Scientific Films

◄ *Very strong jaw muscles and teeth make jaguars the most powerful of big cats, even though tigers and lions are larger.*

The cheetah is the only member of its genus, *Acinonyx*, because scientists are not sure how it is related to other cats.

The puma (also called cougar or mountain lion) is unusual because for a long time its closest relatives were thought to be among the small cats, including house cats, in the genus *Felis*. Scientists use the size and shape of a cat's skull to help decide what genus a species belongs to, so they said that a puma has a house cat's head on a leopard's body. But new studies of their genes suggest to scientists that pumas are in the same line as the *Panthera* cats.

Similar life-style

Closely related or not, the big cats have more in common than large size. All hunt on the ground for large prey such as deer and antelope. All move over very large areas to find enough prey to survive. A single tiger, for example, needs up to 39 square miles (100 square kilometers). All are feared and admired by people.

And all big cats are in danger of extinction. They are hunted for their fur and killed for threatening their human neighbors' cattle. More and more of their wild habitat is being destroyed for farms and ranches. The future of big cats will be decided in your lifetime. These mighty predators will survive only if you know and care about them.

◀ *Pumas, also known as mountain lions or cougars, live in the mountains of western United States and throughout Central and South America. A few pumas also survive in south Florida, where they are called Florida panthers.*

Sized for Siberia

Tigers are the largest cats, and Siberian tigers are the largest tigers. Male tigers in Siberia may grow to more than 13 feet (4 meters) from nose to tail and weigh more than 700 pounds (320 kilograms). Why so big? Scientists think that the bigger a mammal is, the more fat it can store in its body to protect it from the cold. Siberian tigers may get so big because they need a lot of fat to survive Siberia's super-cold winters. In contrast, Sumatran tigers, which live in hot rain forests, weigh only 250 pounds (114 kilograms).

▲ *Except for mothers and their young, tigers usually live and hunt alone. These Siberian tigers have briefly come together to mate.*

Ancestors and relatives

The history of cats begins more than 50 million years ago, with the ancestors of all members of the Carnivora. These ancestors, known as miacids, were small tree-living animals with wide paws, long bodies, long tails, and short flexible limbs.

The evolution of 12 families

About 40 million years ago, one group of miacids became the ancestors of the doglike carnivores. Their descendants are seven of today's families of carnivores: dogs, bears, raccoons, weasels, seals, sea lions, and walruses.

Another group of miacids led to the five families of catlike carnivores. Their living descendants are hyenas, mongooses, genets, and of course cats. The fifth family of catlike carnivores, called nimravids, became extinct about 5 million years ago. Fossils show that the nimravids looked and probably behaved much like cats, although they were not closely related. It is interesting that the nimravids had saber teeth, because this feature also developed in some cats (now extinct). A saber-toothed nimravid called *Dinictus* lived in North America during the Oligocene (37 to 26 million years ago), where it hunted small mammals.

The first cats in the family Felidae appeared during the Miocene (26 to

▼ *About 20,000 years ago, saber-toothed cats fed on a horse near what is now the city of Los Angeles, California. See the tar covering their feet. Lots of animals were trapped and died in the tar pits, where their bones were slowly fossilized.*

Tooth and pouch

During the Pleistocene (2 million to 10,000 years ago), a huge saber-toothed "lion" lived in Australia. Called *Thylacoleo*, it looked and acted like a big cat, but it was a marsupial (a pouched mammal) just like its prey! Its closest relatives alive today are phalangers, small fruit-eating marsupials that live in trees.

Frank Knight/Museum of Victoria

George C. Page Museum

7 million years ago), and by about 10 million years ago modern cats had evolved. We know from fossils that true saber-toothed cats began to emerge during the Pliocene (7 to 2 million years ago), and they flourished in the Pleistocene (2 million to 10,000 years ago). Other cats without saber teeth also lived during the Pleistocene period: lions and tigers, which are still with us; and other species, which became extinct about 10,000 years ago.

The last, and best-known, saber-toothed cat was *Smilodon fatalis*. About the size of a lion, *Smilodon* was an Ice Age cat of North and South America. Its saber teeth were narrow, about 6 inches (15 centimeters) long, and had finely serrated edges. These teeth were easily broken, so *Smilodon* had to be careful when attacking its prey—young mammoths, horses, and other large hoofed mammals. It stabbed and slashed the prey's skin and muscles with its saber teeth but had to keep the teeth from hitting hard bones. Scientists think that *Smilodon* grabbed the side of the prey with its powerful front limbs and claws, then turned the prey over to pierce its soft underbelly.

Smilodon became extinct about 10,000 years ago, at the same time as other Ice Age mammals, such as mammoths, dire wolves, and many species of horses and rhinos, died out. The first people to live in North America probably hunted the same prey as saber-toothed cats—and may even have scavenged the meat that *Smilodon's* fragile sabers could not remove from bones!

▼ *The skull of* Smilodon fatalis *from Rancho La Brea. This saber-tooth cat's skull is similar in size to that of a male African lion, but its saber teeth are 6 inches (152 millimeters) long.*

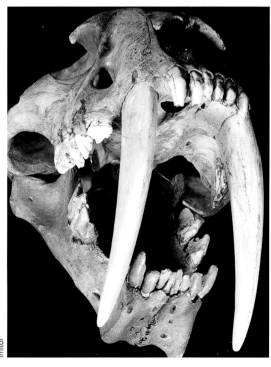

Imitor

◄ *Scientists have found about a million fossil bones of large animals, including big cats, in the Rancho La Brea tar pits near Los Angeles, California.*

How cats work

The big cats hunt and eat vertebrates (animals with backbones), and most of the features that make cats distinct are perfect for this predatory life-style.

▼ *Compared to overall body size, the cheetah's skull is smaller than that of other big cats. Cheetahs also have smaller canine teeth and larger nostrils than other big cats.*

A body designed for speed

The skeleton and muscles of a big cat are like a machine designed for efficient movement to catch and kill prey. Some features are adapted for speed. For example, cats have rather long legs and therefore a long step-length (how much ground is covered with each step). Their stance gives extra length, because the feet are elevated, and only the toes touch the ground. Step-length is also increased by the position of the shoulder blades on the sides of the body, rather than on the back (as in humans), so the shoulders "swing" with the legs.

Cats have a very flexible spine. During a high-speed chase the belly muscles tighten, making the spine arch like a taut bow, so when the muscles relax the cat has explosive power for the next step. It happens so fast that you may not notice the arching of the spine. A long, flexible tail acts like a rudder to improve balance.

The skull

A big cat's skull has short, powerful jaws, with large jaw muscles. Big cats have 30 teeth, 15 on each side of the skull: three upper incisors and three lower incisors, one upper canine and one lower canine, three upper premolars and two lower premolars, one upper molar and one lower molar. The canine teeth are large and powerful for use in killing. One set of premolars is long and bladelike. Cats use these for slicing flesh. None of the teeth is flattened for grinding; only humans and other species that eat an omnivorous diet of meat, fruit, and plants have grinding molars.

Overall, a cat's skull is short, with large openings for eyes placed toward the front. This means that a cat has binocular vision; when it looks at something, it can focus both eyes on the object.

The senses

Sight Large eye openings also mean that a big cat uses mainly vision to find its prey. Large eyes gather more light, which improves the cat's vision at night. Many people believe that cats are color blind, but this is probably not true. Scientists have found that big cats *can* see the color of something that's large or close to them.

Hearing Big cats are believed to have excellent hearing, although scientists have tested only domestic cats for their hearing abilities. Domestic cats are more sensitive to sounds at higher frequencies than humans. Cats can move their ears to locate the source of a sound.

Smell Little is known about cats' sense of smell, or olfaction. They probably do not use smell to find prey, as dogs and bears do. But smell seems to be important when a big cat communicates with other members of its own species. The olfactory system receives smell information through the nostrils (as yours does), but cats also have a vomeronasal olfactory system in which smells travel to the brain through two tiny openings in the roof of the mouth.

Reproductive system

The reproductive system of most cats is basically like humans and many other mammals. A male cat has testicles and, like other carnivores (but unlike humans), a bone called a baculum in the penis. The

---

Spots, stripes, and solids

The big cats are striped (tigers), plain (lions and pumas), or spotted (leopards, jaguars, cheetahs, and snow leopards). Their coat colors are a good camouflage for them, because spots and stripes blend into the shade of forests, while plain coats are less visible in dry open grasslands. But scientists are still puzzled by the differences between the big cats. For instance, why do some have stripes instead of spots?

penis tip is covered with spines, which may stimulate the female to ovulate (release eggs for fertilization) when they mate. Females have up to six pairs of mammary glands for suckling their cubs.

Digestive system

Cats have a simple, short digestive system, much like ours, designed to process meat, which is easily broken down. Unlike dogs, cats cannot tolerate a low-protein diet.

A natural jackknife

When a cat attacks its prey, it uses its sharp claws to control the animal. At other times, the cat usually keeps its claws off the ground, retracted into the feet, to prevent wear on the claws so that they will stay sharp. When needed, the claws are actively extended, or protracted, by stretching a springlike ligament. This is similar to how a jackknife works.

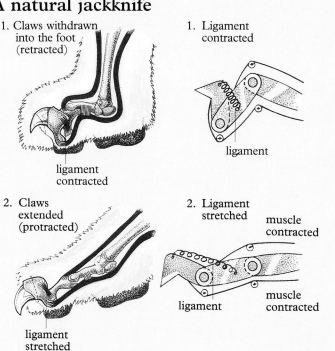

1. Claws withdrawn into the foot (retracted)

ligament contracted

2. Claws extended (protracted)

ligament stretched

1. Ligament contracted

ligament

2. Ligament stretched

muscle contracted

ligament

muscle contracted

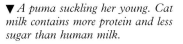

▼ *A puma suckling her young. Cat milk contains more protein and less sugar than human milk.*

The hunters

All big cats are hunters of big game, and their way of hunting is nearly always the same. Big cats hunt on the ground and take advantage of whatever cover there is—tall grass, bushes, trees, and rocks—to approach the prey without being seen.

Closing in for the kill

A cat begins the hunt by selecting its victim, which may be alone or part of a milling herd of hundreds. With its unblinking eyes fixed on the goal, the cat cautiously stalks the prey, moving in a slinking crouch; its ears are flattened, and every muscle is tense. Ever so slowly it moves closer and closer to the prey. Sometimes the cat "freezes" if it sees any sign of fear or alertness in the intended victim. Finally close enough, the cat bursts into a rush to get to the prey, then it pounces, grabs the prey with its paws, and kills it.

Most cats kill by biting the back of the prey's neck with their canine teeth to cut its spinal cord. When killing very large prey, leopards, cheetahs, and tigers usually hold

the prey's throat firmly with their canine teeth until it suffocates. Jaguars sometimes pierce the prey's skull.

Feeding time

After the kill, cats consume their prey immediately if it is small. Lions, which hunt in groups (all of them hungry), consume large prey on the spot. And cheetahs must quickly devour their food before it is stolen by lions, hyenas, or wild dogs.

Other big cats take a more leisurely approach to their dinner. Leopards often pull carcasses up into a tree, where they are safe from scavengers, and feed on them for several days. If a tiger kills in the open, it usually drags the carcass into thick bushes before it begins to feed. Large prey may provide the tiger with meals for three or four days. Jaguars, pumas, and snow leopards treat large prey much as tigers do.

The animals they hunt

All of the big cats prey on hoofed mammals—deer, antelope, wild cattle, wild pigs, wild sheep, zebras, tapirs—depending on what lives where they do. They will take other animals as well, such as monkeys, rodents (rats, mice, and their relatives), rabbits and hares, birds, and even, in the case of jaguars, reptiles and fish.

Lions and tigers, the largest cats, depend on large prey such as wildebeests for lions and axis deer for tigers. These prey are about the same size as or bigger than they are. Although lions and tigers do take smaller prey, they cannot survive on it for long, because they use up more energy when chasing after small prey than the energy-value of the meat on it.

The medium-sized big cats also prefer prey their size or larger, but they can exist on a diet of fairly small rodents and birds when larger hoofed animals are scarce. Snow leopards, for example, prefer wild sheep but sometimes manage on marmots and pheasants. Pumas in the western United States often live on white-tailed deer and elk in the winter and ground squirrels in the summer. Pumas are also remarkable for the size of prey they are able to kill compared to their own body size. For example, a female puma can even kill a bull elk, seven times its own size!

◄ *This lion has selected a single victim among a herd of zebras and is going in for the kill. Zebras can be dangerous targets—sometimes a well-placed kick from the prey can kill the attacking lion.*

Eyes on the prize

Cats have binocular vision—they can focus both eyes on a single object, as you can. This helps them to judge distance, which is important in the hunt.

Cats see much better in the dark than you can. A special part of their eyes reflects light, so the object appears brighter to them. This makes the "eyeshine" of the leopard's eyes in the photograph.

Rafi Ben-Shahar/Oxford Scientific Films

► *A leopard carries the carcass of a gazelle into a tree to keep it away from scavengers. The leopard can pull a carcass that weighs several times more than its own weight.*

The behavior of big cats

Big cats vary in size, live in many different habitats, and hunt different prey, but they are remarkably similar in their behavior.

Time for resting

Most big cats prefer to hunt at night or at dawn and dusk. But their daily activities vary, depending on the season, the weather, and the periods when prey are usually active. Between hunting trips and bouts of feeding, big cats rest and sleep.

When there are lots of large prey, and kills are easy to make, big cats spend much of the day, sometimes several days, resting after gorging on a large meal. When cats must survive on smaller prey that are dispersed over a large area, they spend far more time traveling and hunting. Jaguars living on small prey in the rain forest, for example, may hunt for 16 hours every day. The cats usually rest in the shelter of bushes or trees, especially during the hottest part of the day. All big cats, except for lions and tigers, rest in trees.

Courtship and mating

A male cat knows when a female is coming into estrus (the period when she is ready to mate) by changes in her odors. A few days before the female is ready to mate, the male follows and tries to approach her. He also scent-marks by rubbing his cheeks and neck on objects in the environment. At first the female hisses and bats at the male with her paws, but she also scent-marks and sniffs where the male has left his marks.

Finally the female allows the male to mount and copulate with her. He lightly

▼ *Cheetah cubs fight playfully near their den. Through play, young cats practice hunting skills such as stalking and pouncing. They also rehearse the behavior they will use as adults in fights with other members of their species.*

holds the nape of her neck at the beginning of the mount, then lets go and yowls. After copulation, the female cries out, throws the male off her back, then rolls on her back for a few seconds. The big cats take only a few minutes for mounting and copulation, but a pair may copulate hundreds of times during the female's three-day estrous period. Then male and female go their separate ways.

Jonathan Scott/Planet Earth Pictures

▶ *This male lion is performing a behavior called "flehmen." His upper lip is pulled back in a grimace, and he seems paralyzed, breathing slowly with a staring look. Males do this when sniffing the urine of females to find out if they are ready for mating.*

Anup Shah/Jacana

A female lion mates with all the males in her group, but females in solitary species will mate with only one male.

Maternal care

The pregnant female seeks out a sheltered den in thick bushes to give birth. The young are born blind and helpless; their eyes open at about two weeks of age. They stay in the den until they are six to eight weeks old, while their mother divides her time between nursing them in the den and hunting. Then the young start to go with her on hunting trips and are soon weaned.

Mothers often bring prey to the den area so the young can begin to practice the killing bite. This is the hardest part of hunting behavior for them to learn. During the next year or two, the young stay with their mother while they develop their hunting skills.

Cats at play

When cubs play they are practicing the skills they will use to survive as adults. Cubs play-fight, wrestling with and stalking each other to practice stalking and taking down prey. Scientists think they do this while still in the den and continue to play-fight while their little teeth and claws cannot do much damage. Later the young practice stalking, rushing, and pouncing on other objects, just like domestic kittens playing with a ball of string or a toy mouse.

Gunter Ziesler/Bruce Coleman Ltd

Q. What is a lion's favorite pastime?

A. Sleeping. A well-fed lion may sleep 19 hours out of every 24. And with no predators to worry about, lions rest easy. They often sleep recklessly sprawled out in the shade of a tree.

17

Communication

Big cats communicate with each other in a variety of ways. As most of them are solitary animals, they must be able to communicate over long distances, as well as when they are face to face.

Communicating from a distance

All of the big cats leave scent-marks, which reveal information about an individual's sex, reproductive status, identity, and occupation of a particular area. The odorous substances are in cat urine, feces, and saliva, and they are also produced by special glands on the tail, chin, and lips. Cats spray urine or rub the glands on trees and other plants, usually at the height of another cat's head. Some big cats make scrapes of vegetation on which they urinate and defecate. Some also rake their claws across the bark of trees, leaving visible marks as well as odors from sweat glands on their paws. Other cats of the same species "read" these signals. Thus cats can communicate with each other without ever meeting.

Lions, tigers, leopards, and jaguars also communicate at a distance through loud calls that may carry more than a mile.

Close calls

At short distances, big cats use several different sounds to communicate about their intentions or mood. All big cats make a "meow" call, used most often between mothers and young. In a louder form, females may meow to attract mates.

In friendly situations, big cats make a soft but noisy sound as a greeting. In lions and leopards, this is a puffing sound, but

▲ *A lion sniffs a female to see if she is ready for mating. If she is not, she swipes her paw and bares her teeth. If she is, she allows the male to come close.*

▼ *Sound is only one way in which cats communicate. All cats can "meow," but not all cats can roar. This puma is making a high, whistlelike meow.*

Zefa-BAUER

tigers, jaguars, and snow leopards make a snorting sound called prusten. During aggressive meetings, big cats hiss, growl, and spit, and a cat being attacked may shriek. Pumas purr, which is usually a signal between a mother and her kittens that says "all is well." No one knows whether the other big cats purr.

When big cats call, they also make different facial expressions and body postures. This is most clearly seen in aggressive interactions. An aggressive cat on the offensive growls and rotates its ears forward, stands with its back parallel to the ground or its weight shifted to its front legs, and swings its tail from side to side. At the other extreme, a submissive or defensive cat hisses, flattens its ears, dilates its pupils, and may slink away, crouch down, or even roll over on its back.

Scent communication is important when two big cats come together. A male, for instance, sniffs the rear end of a female coming into estrus, then bares his teeth in flehmen behavior. Male and female sometimes rub necks when a female is in estrus and ready for mating; this may show their "friendly" intentions.

◀ *A defensive leopard—ears laid back, pupils constricted, and teeth bared.*

▼ *This snow leopard is also on the defensive, as shown by its flattened ears, nearly closed eyes, and open mouth.*

Why do lions roar?

A male lion's roar may be as loud as 114 decibels, louder than the call of any other big cat. Both male and female lions roar in several different situations. A lion may roar to make contact with other members of its group (called a pride) or to find any member of its species. Within a pride, several lions often roar together, perhaps to strengthen the bond between members of the pride. A pride may also roar together to announce its ownership of a territory if another pride is nearby.

Lions

The king of beasts once ranged over a huge part of the Earth. Until about 10,000 years ago, lions lived in North America and northern South America, throughout Africa, in Europe and the Middle East, and as far as southern India and the island of Sri Lanka. Since then, the lion's range has steadily become smaller and smaller.

▼ Most of the world's lions live in Africa south of the Sahara, but about 300 cling to survival in a reserve in northwest India.

More people, fewer lions

Today, lions are found in Africa between the southern edge of the Sahara desert and Botswana. One small population of about 300 lions continues to survive in a reserve called the Gir Forest in northwest India. This is all that is left of the lion's kingdom.

Lions are the best known of the big cats, to the public as well as to scientists. Adult lions have plain, unspotted, light brown coats. Male lions grow a mane around the face, and this becomes darker and fuller as the male gets older. Adult males weigh between 330 and 550 pounds (150–250 kilograms) and are 48 inches (123 centimeters) high at the shoulder. Females are usually smaller, weighing between 264 to 400 pounds (120–182 kilograms). Females are about 6 inches (16 centimeters) shorter than males.

Cubs are born with spots on their coats that gradually fade away as they grow up. A female has as many as four cubs, which are born after a 110-day gestation period. A newborn cub weighs about 3 pounds 5 ounces (1.5 kilograms) and is blind and helpless. Cubs rely on their mothers until about two years of age, when they are nearly adult size.

▲ Female lions are good mothers and tolerate the playful antics of their young cubs. They are also good aunts and help to look after any cubs in the pride.

Purdy & Matthews/Survival Anglia

Asian and African

The Asian lion and the African lion are subspecies. This means that scientists see differences between them, but they are not as different as a lion and a tiger, or a lion and a leopard. The Asian lion has a flap of skin on its abdomen, called a belly fold, that the African lion never has. The mane of a male African lion is much thicker and fuller on top of its head than the Asian lion's mane. Scientists also find differences in the shape of the skull between the two subspecies of lions.

Home and habitat

African lions live in groups called prides. Males, females, and young make up a pride. As you will read later, lions are the most social of all the cats, big and small. African lions always live in open areas, such as the savanna grasslands of East Africa, the dry woodlands south of the Sahara, and even treeless parts of the Kalahari desert.

A pride of lions defends a large area, called a territory, from other prides and any individual lions that might enter the area. The size of a pride's territory depends on how many prey animals—such as zebras, wildebeests, and buffalo—live in the area. It also depends on the number of lions in the pride. In East Africa, the territory sizes are from 8 to 154 square miles (20 to 400 square kilometers).

The lions of India's Gir Forest, called Asian lions, live in more wooded habitats (wild places with more trees) than African lions. Unlike African lions, males and females do not live together in prides. During the dry season, female Asian lions stay among the trees along rivers, but males are rarely seen there. In the monsoon season when it's hot and raining much of the time, males are seen on dry open hilltops, where the wind keeps away insects. Females avoid these open areas.

The future of lions

The range of lions in Africa is still shrinking. People kill lions for sport or to protect their cattle. As the human population grows in Africa, more and more of the lions' habitat is taken over for ranches and other human activities. This may mean that lions cannot leave an area to mate or find food because they are surrounded by people. When this happens, inbreeding (mating between close relatives) may reduce the number of young that are born. Inbreeding may also increase the number of cubs that die soon after birth. Lions still exist in good numbers in some parts of Africa. But unless people change their ways, the king of beasts may soon rule no more.

Hunters and scavengers

Lions have an ancient reputation as great hunters. They are second only to tigers in size, and hunting in groups gives them extra power. But studies of lions in East Africa show that lions make a kill only once in every five attempts—the other four times the prey gets away!

▼ *The ears of a male Asian lion, such as the one below, can always be seen between its short mane, but an African lion's ears are usually hidden by its fuller, longer mane.*

Lions also scavenge food that is killed by other predators. They watch the movement of vultures, which hover over kills, and listen for the calls of feeding hyenas to lead them to food. Lions then scare hyenas, cheetahs, leopards, and other small carnivores away from their hard-won prey and eat whatever the others have left. When prey and other predators are plentiful, lions may get half of their food by scavenging.

Male lions also scrounge food from the females in their pride. Females do most of the hunting in lion prides. When female lions make a kill, the males quickly move in. Because they are bigger and stronger than females, the males eat first. Adult females eat next, then younger, juvenile lions. The youngest cubs are the last to eat. As a result, many cubs starve when prey is scarce. Usually only a very large kill will provide enough meat for all members of the pride.

Lions' favorite prey are medium-sized hoofed mammals such as zebras and wildebeests. If a lion preyed only on zebras and wildebeests it would need to kill about 30 of these animals each year to stay alive. But lions hunting in groups can kill very large animals such as buffalo, giraffes, and even small elephants. They also catch small animals like hares and gazelles, which are just enough for a meal.

Scientists call lions "opportunistic" hunters. This means lions will eat whatever they can catch for themselves or steal from other predators. We would call lions lazy. They would rather scavenge than hunt a meal, and between meals they rest. In fact, lions rest about 19 hours of the day.

But a lion's life is not always easy. A zebra's powerful kick with its hoof can kill a lion trying to catch it. Elephants, buffalo,

J. Bracegirdle/Planet Earth Pictures

Stuffed!

An adult lion needs about 11 pounds (5 kilograms) of meat a day to stay alive. But lions do not eat three meals a day every day of the week. A lion may eat up to 77 pounds (35 kilograms) in one meal, then rest for several days before hunting or scavenging again.

and rhinos can also kill lions that threaten them. Left alone while their mother hunts, lion cubs may be killed by leopards, jackals, and wild dogs. Male lions often die in fights with other males that are trying to take over a pride of females. And a group of hyenas or jackals can steal a meal from a male lion hunting alone. In the wild, male lions rarely live longer than 12 years, while females sometimes get to be 16 or older.

▲ *Lions steal food from jackals and other predators whenever they can. Sometimes half of what lions eat comes from scavenging.*

▼ *All alone, this huge male lion may lose its dinner to the group of jackals closing in on its kill. The hyena lurking in the background could also steal the lion's kill.*

Frans Lanting/Minden Pictures

▲ *A male lion brings down a wildebeest with its powerful forelimbs, before killing it by biting through the bones in the wildebeest's neck.*

Most sociable of cats

Unlike most cats, lions are usually found with companions. Adult female lions can hunt and survive alone, but they do well only when they are part of a group. Because they are poorer hunters than females, lone males rarely survive at all.

A group of lions is called a pride. Five or six adult females, two to four adult males, and cubs make up a typical pride of about 15 lions. The important thing about a pride is that all of the females are related. Mothers, daughters, sisters, aunts, and cousins stay together for their entire lives. Because females stay together in the area where they are born, a pride's territory belongs to the female lions. The females defend the territory from other female lions and from strange males. Unrelated females almost never form a pride or join an existing one.

Female relatives hunt together and share their kills. They defend their territory together and are friendly with others in the pride. Females also help each other raise their nieces and nephews.

The life of a male lion

Because life is so hard for single male lions, they do sometimes team up with one or two unrelated males. But more often, the males in a pride are brothers, half-brothers, or cousins and about the same age. These males are not, however, related to the females in their pride.

When young males are between two and four years old, they are driven out of the area where they were born. If a male is

◀ *Close association between cubs may last all their lives. Females stay in the pride of their birth. Males strike out to find a new pride.*

Jonathan Scott/Planet Earth Pictures

▼ *Lion cubs begin following their mother on hunting trips when they are a few months old, but they are usually the last to eat when a kill is made.*

Day care in cats

Mother lions whose cubs were born at about the same time are able to leave them together in a lion "nursery" while they go off to hunt. Any mother who stays behind will protect the cubs in the nursery. A few years later, the females who were raised together in the nursery will help each other to look after their own cubs.

Matthews & Purdy/Survival Anglia

lucky, he will go with plenty of brothers and male cousins to hunt with, until he finds a pride of females to join. In fact, scientists think that females in a pride give birth at about the same time to give their sons this advantage in life. (This also helps daughters, whose own cubs will have aunts to look after them.) An unlucky male lion must leave alone, and unless he soon finds a companion he may starve to death or be killed by a group of males.

To join a pride of females, a group of males must usually win a battle with the males already living among the females. Most of the time, the battle is won by the larger group of males. Young males can often beat old ones. Males sometimes die in the bloody fights, but the winners take all. They can now share in the food the females kill, and they can begin to father cubs of their own. Males also have duties in the pride. They help to defend the territory against unwanted male intruders, and they protect their young cubs.

But the good life in a pride does not last very long for a male group. Usually within two to four years, another group of males in search of a pride will be big enough or strong enough to take over the females. Without females, the defeated males have a hard time hunting. They are often injured by zebras and wildebeests. When they lose their health or their teeth, or lose a teammate, they soon die.

Living in a pride with lions of all ages, females fare much better. Even an old, nearly toothless female, no longer able to hunt, shares in the kills made by her daughters and nieces as long as she can keep up with them. This behavior is seen in no other cat species. Lions are truly the most social of cats.

▼ *Imagine you are the young lion labeled 15. The other lions in the pride are: 1 father's brother, 2 father's half-brother, 3 father, 4 aunt, 5 grandmother, 6 mother's half-sister, 7 great aunt, 8 brother, 9 sister, 10 mother, 11 mother's half-sister, 12 half-sister, 13 cousin, 14 cousin.*

▶ *These males have come across females and cubs feeding. Even though the female lions made the kill, the bigger, stronger males can drive them away. The females then must wait until the males have had their fill at the carcass.*

Jonathan Scott/Planet Earth Pictures

Tigers

Tigers once ranged throughout Asia, from icy-cold Siberia to the hot, humid rain forests of Southeast Asia.

Eight different types

Scientists think the first tigers appeared in China. Over hundreds of thousands of years, as tigers roamed further into different parts of Asia, they developed into eight subspecies. Separated from each other by seas or mountain ranges, the subspecies changed in size, color, and stripe pattern.

Extinct or endangered

Sadly, three of the eight subspecies are now extinct, and the others are endangered.

What happened to this great predator? One thing is the use of modern guns. People have always admired the tiger's beautiful fur. Many also believe that parts of the tiger, such as its tail, can be ground into a medicine to cure diseases. And people have always feared tigers, which sometimes kill livestock and people themselves. But only the bravest of the brave ever hunted a tiger. It was just too dangerous.

Modern weapons changed all that. It is easy for a person with a gun to hunt and kill a tiger, so in the past 100 years tigers have been killed in great numbers out of human greed or fear. During the same time, more and more people moved into the tiger's habitats in Asia, clearing the land for farms and villages, and hunting the wild animals that tigers need to survive. In the past 20 to 30 years many laws have been passed to help tigers. But laws came too late to save some subspecies.

The Bali tiger was the first to become extinct, in the 1940s. It lived only on the small island of Bali in Indonesia, was the smallest subspecies, and had the darkest coat color. Next to go were the tigers of Java, another Indonesian island; the last Javan tigers died out in the 1980s. So did the Caspian tiger of central Eurasia.

Only a few Chinese tigers exist, and they may be gone by the time you read this. Chinese tigers are the oldest subspecies and have fewer stripes than any of the others. Only about 500 Sumatran tigers, another island subspecies in Indonesia, survive in the wild. Sumatran tigers have rich reddish coats and long ruffs of hair around their faces. They are now the world's smallest living tigers. The largest subspecies, the Siberian tiger, also exists in very low numbers. Little is known about the Indo-Chinese tigers of Laos, Thailand, and Vietnam, but scientists believe they too are nearly gone.

Q. What are white tigers?

A. Some people think that the white tigers they see in zoos are Siberian tigers, but it is not true. They are not a tiger subspecies. White tigers are a mutant form, which happens very rarely in the wild. In the past, many zoos interbred tigers that had genes for whiteness, to produce more white tigers. Most modern zoos no longer do this because white tigers have no role in conservation efforts.

▼ *Tigers are the only big cats with stripes. The subspecies of tigers have slightly different coat colors and amounts of striping. A dark orange coat and moderate striping tell us that this is a Bengal tiger.*

Saving the tiger

In this sad story, only the status of the Bengal tiger gives hope for the survival of tigers in the wild. In 1900, about 40,000 Bengal tigers lived in India, but by 1972, only about 2000 were left. In 1973, conservation groups from around the world joined the government of India to start "Project Tiger." Its motto was "Save the Tiger."

Laws were passed to stop tiger hunting and to stop the international trade of tiger skins. Areas where tigers still lived were turned into nature reserves to protect tigers and their prey. People were not allowed to take over the tigers' habitat in the reserves for farms or cattle grazing. Today the number of tigers in India is about 4000—twice as many as 30 years ago. But Bengal tigers, like the others, are still in danger. Their survival depends on stopping illegal hunting and on people learning to make a living without using the tigers' habitat.

▼ *Tigers will survive in the wild if people learn how to live near tigers without killing them or being killed.*

The family life of a loner

Tigers are loners most of the time, but they do have a social life. Males and females get together to mate. Cubs live with their mothers for a long time after their birth. Tigers also know their neighbors and keep track of their movements, even though they avoid meeting face to face.

A female tiger lives, hunts, and raises her young in the same large area. She "owns" this area, or territory, and tries to keep other females out. Sometimes two female neighbors fight at the boundaries of their territories. A territory owner may also fight with a female looking for a place to live. Usually females would rather avoid each other, because fighting is so dangerous.

Females scent-mark bushes and trees on the boundaries with urine and feces, and they put scratch-marks on trees. These smells and scratches are messages that say to other females, "Do not enter. This is my area." Neighbors also get to know each other through the smells. A female sniffing around the boundary can tell whether her neighbor has been nearby or whether a new female has entered the area.

Male tigers also live on territories, which they defend from other males. Like females, they use scent-marks and scratches to tell other males to keep out. But males will fight over territorial ownership because a male's territory gives him more than a place to live and hunt. It also gives him the chance to be a father. A male tiger's large territory usually overlaps the smaller territories of two or more females, with which he mates. A male tiger will fight to expand his territory to include more females. Territorial males are often challenged by young males looking for a territory and females to mate with.

Male and female tigers change their movements so they aren't in an area at the same time unless a female is in estrus (ready to mate). Both the male and the female leave scent-mark messages about where they are so they can avoid each other. The female's scent-marks also tell the male when she is in estrus. The estrous smell says, "Let's get together."

A male and female stay together for a few days during mating, but the job of raising cubs is the female's alone. She will usually have two or three cubs every two to three years. Cubs are born blind and helpless. Their mother stays with them all the time for a few days, and after that she leaves them alone just for short periods while she hunts. Cubs depend entirely on their mother's milk until they are six to eight weeks old. At this time, the female begins to take her cubs to animals she has killed, so that they can eat meat.

Mother and cubs are rarely apart for the next year. It takes a long time for tigers to learn to be good enough hunters to live on their own. Finally, by about 18 months of age, the young tigers spend hours and days away from their mother and are making some of their own kills. But they use their mother's territory for another year or so.

When do the young leave their mother completely? This depends on when her next cubs are born. Usually older cubs stay around until the new cubs begin to go to kills with the mother. When they leave, they try to find an area to make a territory and begin the loner's life as an adult tiger.

Gerard Lacz/NHPA

▲ A tiger cub "attacks" a branch to practice its hunting skills. It takes tigers a long time to learn to become good hunters.

◄ A tiger mother and her cubs stay close together until the cubs are more than a year old. A female may have one, two, or three cubs at a time.

▶ If water is in short supply, adult tigers may drink and cool down in the same place. A male may join a female or a female may join another female, but two males seldom get together peacefully.

Anup Shah/Planet Earth Pictures

What's for lunch?

Tigers take prey as small as hog deer, about 65 pounds (30 kilograms), or as huge as the gaur (an Asian species in the cow family), which weighs up to 2000 pounds (910 kilograms). A favorite of tigers in Nepal is sambar, a large Asian deer weighing about 400 pounds (180 kilograms), but they also take smaller chital (spotted deer) and wild pigs. Of the hoofed mammals in their range, only adult rhinos and the mighty elephants are safe from becoming a tiger's lunch!

A camera in tigerland

Tigers live in the shadows, roaming mostly at night through the deep, dark forest. Photographs of resting tigers taken in sunlight do not really capture the beauty of these night hunters. But it's hard for a photographer to even *find* a tiger in the dark far less take its picture. So two scientists studying tigers in Nepal figured out how to get tigers to take pictures of themselves!

First they guessed where a tiger might be traveling on a particular night. Then they found a place along the guessed-at tiger path to hide a camera. Finally, they had to make a device to trigger a motor-driven camera and the flashlight when a tiger was in the camera's field of view. After many failures, they found that a buried plate, connected by a cable to the camera, worked best. When a tiger stepped on the plate, the pressure made the plate hit a switch that set off the camera.

The system wasn't foolproof. Unless the tiger came along the path in the right direction, all they got was a shot of its rear end. If the tiger stepped on the plate with a hindfoot instead of a forefoot, the photo was out of focus. The scientists were surprised that the tigers didn't seem to mind the flash but hated the buzzing noise of the motor-drive. Once a tiger heard that sound, it would not return to the area for weeks. Other animals also set off the camera, and sometimes the flash didn't go off.

In the first seven months, the tigers took lots of photos but only three really good ones! Still, the scientists kept trying.

Tigers turned out to be quite bad photographers. But over the years, even the bad photographs helped scientists to learn a lot about the tigers that move at night in the forests of Nepal.

▲ *Tigers often ambush prey when they come to a waterhole to drink. This tiger has killed a sambar, a large Asian deer.*

Belinda Wright/DRK Photo

motor-driven camera

camera flash
covered in plastic

6-volt battery

cable

pressure plate

▲ *This tiger is about to take its own picture. When it steps on the plate, its weight will trigger the camera, which is hidden in the bushes.*

The life of a tigress

No one knows exactly when Chuchchi was born, but she died on the afternoon of August 10, 1987. For 15 years this tigress had lived in the forest of Nepal's Chitwan National Park. At that time, more was known about her than about any other wild tiger. In fact, much of what you read about tiger behavior is based on what scientists learned from studying her.

Chuchchi lived on the same territory for 10 years. In this time, seven different males shared this area—some for just a few months. Three males stayed long enough to father her cubs. Her first cubs were born in 1975, when she was about three years old, and her last cubs in 1985. In these 10 years, she had a total of 16 young. Eleven of her cubs survived until they were at least two years old and moved away.

From Chuchchi and her family, scientists learned that daughters often stay close to their mother. A daughter born in 1977 settled in a territory next to Chuchchi's. A few years later, Chuchchi gave up half of her own territory to another daughter. In 1986, a third daughter took over her mother's territory and drove Chuchchi out of it.

After this, Chuchchi did not have her own home range to live and hunt in. She wandered far to places she had never been. But she always went back to her home area, where she was finally killed by the three-year-old son of a female who had been Chuchchi's neighbor in the forest. After watching Chuchchi for more than 12 years, the scientists knew her so well that they felt as though they had lost a friend. They still miss the tigress that taught them so much.

▲ *Chuchchi, whose name means "pointed toes," was a favorite of tiger watchers in Nepal. They followed her life just as many people follow the lives of movie stars.*

Leopards

Leopards live throughout Africa, through the Middle East, Asia Minor, South and Southeast Asia, and on the Asian continent. They even live on small islands like Zanzibar, off the east coast of Africa, and Sri Lanka, off the southern tip of India.

▼ *Usually solitary, these leopards have come together to mate in a very unusual watery habitat.*

The most adaptable cats

Author Rudyard Kipling was impressed with the leopard's changeable nature, as this passage in "How the Leopard Got its Spots" from *Just So Stories* shows:

"Now you are a beauty!" said the Ethiopian. "You can lie out on the bare ground and look like a heap of pebbles. You can lie out on the naked rocks and look like a piece of pudding-stone. You can lie out on a leafy branch and look like sunshine sifting through the leaves; and you can lie right across the center of a path and look like nothing in particular."

Leopards do have an amazing ability to blend into their surroundings—so much so that leopards often live, unknown to their human neighbors, in the suburbs of African cities such as Nairobi. This may help to explain the leopard's very large range, throughout Africa and Asia.

◄ Leopards spend about two-thirds of their time resting and watching the world around them. They often do this up in a tree.

This includes diverse habitats, from near-desert and rocky mountains to grasslands and rain forests and agricultural lands. Leopards are at home in all of them. They prefer some cover of vegetation, but are not afraid to cross wide-open areas. Where leopards are the only big cats, they are bold and aggressive. But when they share their habitat with tigers and lions, they take a more cautious approach to life to avoid fatal encounters with the larger cats.

Skilled in many ways

Leopards eat whatever prey is available, from very small rodents to very large wildebeests. They will also scavenge from other predators. You might say they specialize in being generalists. This also shows up in their body plan. Leopards are average big cats. They are four times smaller than tigers and lions, and four times larger than clouded leopards. They aren't streamlined runners like cheetahs, or stocky powerhouses like jaguars. They aren't mountain climbers like snow leopards. Leopards just do everything well enough to survive under a variety of conditions.

As a result, leopards have fared better in the modern world than tigers or lions. But that is beginning to change.

The threat from humans

Leopard numbers seem to be declining. Leopards are now threatened or endangered throughout their range. People used to hunt leopards for sport and fur, until they were protected in most places about 20 years ago, but illegal hunting continues.

Leopards also learn quickly to prey on farmers' livestock, for which they often receive the death sentence. If a leopard is disturbed while eating its kill, it will usually return later and does not mind eating carrion (rotting flesh). This makes it easy for people to poison them. So it seems that the behavior that makes them survivors in the natural world may now make them losers in the civilized world.

Did you know?

Male leopards weigh between 81 and 198 pounds (37–90 kilograms). Females are about a third smaller, at 62 to 132 pounds (28–60 kilograms). A large size difference between males and females is typical of big cats.

► A leopard cub feeds on a gazelle carcass, which its mother has stored in a tree. In the tree, both cub and carcass are protected from predators and scavengers such as lions, hyenas, and wild dogs.

How much space does a leopard need?

An adult leopard lives and hunts in a home range that provides enough food and shelter to satisfy its needs. The size depends on the habitat. For example, in the forests of Nepal where there are many hoofed mammals to prey on, a leopard's home range might be as small as 2¼ square miles (6 square kilometers). In East African grasslands, leopards at some times need only 4¼ square miles (11 square kilometers), but they may need 46 square miles (120 square kilometers). And in the barren mountains of southern Africa, one male leopard ranged over 188 square miles (487 square kilometers)!

It is common among all big cats (and other carnivores) that individuals in some habitats have small territories while in other habitats they need a large territory, but the leopard is the only species with such a great difference between the smallest home ranges and the largest.

▶ *This leopard has found a good branch to rest on. It will hunt on the ground but may drag the carcass up into a tree before eating it.*

▼ *Leopards carefully stalk their prey until they are close enough to rush at the animal and grab it by the throat.*

Stephen J. Krasemann/DRK Photo

Leopards and our ancestors

Leopards seldom eat people, but during the Pleistocene (2 million to 10,000 years ago) our ancestors often became a meal for a hungry leopard. As far as the leopards were concerned, humans (and some of our early ancestors, called hominids) were as easy to catch as any other primate. Today, leopards often eat primates such as langurs and colobus monkeys, especially in those areas where hoofed mammals are scarce.

Scientists in South Africa have dug up the fossil skull of one early hominid in a cave. In the skull there are two small holes, which were probably made by the canine teeth of a leopard whose skull was found in the same cave. The scientists think the leopard killed the hominid and stored the body in a tree near the cave's mouth, so the bones fell into the cave. Later, the bones of the leopard fell into the cave as well. Or it could be that a couple of hominids, searching for their friend, killed the leopard.

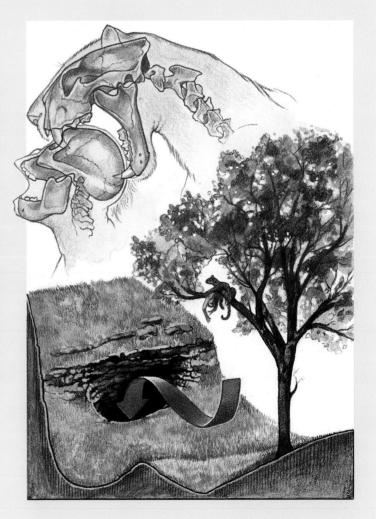

▶ *Did it happen like this? We can only guess!*

34

Predator and prey!

This leopard is intently watching something—perhaps a distant baboon troop. In Africa, leopards prey on baboons at night, when the baboons are most vulnerable. But in the daytime, baboons climb trees to steal the meat that leopards store there. A troop of baboons can drive away an adult leopard, and male baboons sometimes kill and eat leopard cubs. Leopards may have lived (and died) with our ancestors just as they do today with baboons.

Social life

Leopards are flexible in their social life. Each one lives alone on its home range (except for mothers and young), but in some places the home ranges of individuals may overlap. In Nepal, for example, each female leopard seems to defend her home range from other females, so there is little or no overlap; males, too, are territorial, but each one's territory overlaps with several females. In Sri Lanka, however, one male and one female may share a single territory around a water hole. And in Thailand, the home ranges of several males and females may be almost the same.

A mother and her young

A female leopard gives birth to two or three young in a secluded den among thick vegetation. Cubs weigh about 1 pound (500 grams) at birth, and they open their eyes for the first time on the tenth day.

Q. What is a black panther?

A. *Black panther* is the name sometimes given to a leopard that is melanistic—which means the background color of its coat is black. But it is not a different species. Sometimes a black cub is born in the same litter as yellowish cubs. And even a black leopard has spots; you just can't see them among the dark fur. Black leopards are most common in rain forest habitats.

When scientists in Nepal watched a female leopard, they saw her move her cubs from one den to another during the first six weeks, until the cubs were old enough to follow her. While the cubs were in a den, the mother alternated between cub care and hunting. She sometimes spent three days away and then three days with them. She often needed to spend such a long time away because she had to hunt and kill prey and stay with the carcass until she finished eating it. Otherwise it would rot in the hot climate or be stolen by scavengers.

The young stay with their mother until they are between 16 months and two years of age. Then they leave, to live on their own. Some travel a long distance to find a new home. Others, male or female, may live alone on their mother's territory or stay in a neighboring area for a while. We do not know if these homebodies stay near their mothers to have their own families, or move somewhere else. However, you can bet that leopards will do whatever works best.

◄ *From the vantage point of a tree, a leopard surveys the African plains.*

▶ *A young leopard waiting and watching. It is usual for a leopard to leave its mother between 16 months and two years of age. Some wander far away, others stay near or in their mother's territory.*

Stephen J. Krasemann/DRK Photo

Row A
Row B
Row C
Row D
Row E

Mark Deeble & Victoria Stone

How to tell a leopard by its spots

All leopards have spots on their face, but some have more spots than others. Some have lines of spots under their eyes, while other leopards wear a "necklace" of spots under the throat. Spots on the forehead may form circles, ovals, or squares. They're all different. Does a spot-pattern identify an individual leopard, the way that fingerprints identify individual people?

The answer is: very nearly. When studying leopards, scientists can almost always recognize individuals by their spots. They say that a leopard's face spots are almost as distinctive as human facial features. The best clues come from comparing the number of spots in rows D, C, and B.

Jaguars

Long ago, giant jaguars used to roam throughout North America. The modern jaguar is much smaller than its ancestor, and it is not as widespread. It now lives only in Mexico, Central America, and South America as far as northern Argentina.

Largest cat in tropical America

The largest modern jaguar may reach 300 pounds (136 kilograms) in weight, but most of them weigh much less. The average weight for a male is 121 pounds (55 kilograms), and for a female 79 pounds (36 kilograms). The head and body length is 6 feet (185 centimeters) maximum. Jaguars and leopards are similar in size and color, but jaguars are stockier and more powerful. Jaguars have short, thick legs and large feet; a short back; a large head; and very wide

Jaguars often rest on tree limbs that reach over the edge of a river.

Loren McIntyre

38

Predator and predator

This jaguar's prey is a young black caiman. Black caimans may grow to almost 20 feet (6 meters) in length, which makes them the largest predator in South America.

Jaguars eat caimans, but both species suffer from a common enemy—skin traders. Jaguars are killed so their beautiful spotted fur can be fashioned into coats. Black caimans are killed so their distinctively marked skins can be transformed into leather for purses and shoes. As a result, both species are endangered.

Loren McIntyre

▲ *This jaguar cub's prey is a small caiman. Jaguars are the only big cats that regularly eat caimans and other reptiles.*

▲ *The fur of jaguars varies in color from pale gold to rich rusty red. All-black (melanistic) jaguars are not uncommon.*

39

canine teeth. Some people say that leopards are built like runners, while jaguars are built like heavyweight wrestlers.

Jaguars are creatures of thick forests. They sometimes travel into grassland to find prey but always return to the forest for most of the day. The type of forest does not seem to matter. They live in vast rain forests, or in strips of forest along rivers, or even in thorny thickets of bush. Within the forest, jaguars are usually found near water. They can swim wide rivers and often travel along riverbanks. They also choose waterside spots to rest and to find prey.

A solitary life

We do not know much about the jaguar's social life, but they seem to be typical solitary big cats. Each female lives alone (or with her cubs) on a home range of 4 to 27 square miles (10–70 square kilometers). The home range of a male is two or three times larger, and it overlaps the ranges of several females. Young ones share their mother's range until they are about two years old. When home ranges overlap, jaguars avoid hunting in the same area.

What do jaguars eat?

Tapirs, which are hoofed mammals related to horses and rhinos, are the only large prey species available; they are usually twice as

Werner Forman Archive/Dallas Museum of Fine Art

big as the jaguar. Like most other forest animals, tapirs live alone or in pairs and are widely scattered. As a result, jaguars hunt a great variety of smaller species. They take whatever animals are common in their local

▼ *At birth a jaguar cub weighs less than 2 pounds (900 grams). It may have two or three brothers and sisters in the same litter.*

Alan & Sandy Carey

area and eat almost anything they come across in their travels.

Jaguars prefer to eat peccaries (a species of pig) and capybara (the world s largest rodent), which are unusual among rain forest animals because they live in groups. But a jaguar s diet might also include deer, opossums, monkeys, squirrels, small birds, fish, reptiles, and even tiny morsels such as snails. In Belize, a country in Central America, jaguars eat mostly armadillos.

Jaguars can t afford to be fussy eaters in the forest, but the ability to eat virtually anything gets them into trouble with people. Jaguars quickly learn to prey on horses and cows when ranchers move into their habitat, so ranchers usually try to kill all the jaguars in the area. People living in the rain forest depend on the same species as jaguars do for meat, so hunters also kill any jaguar they meet there. As human populations grow, jaguar populations are being reduced or becoming extinct.

▲ *This drawing of a jaguar is from* Lloyd's Natural History, *published in 1896.*

A taste for turtles

A jaguar can kill a large mammal by a powerful bite to the head or neck, and is the only cat to regularly kill by piercing the prey s skull. But it can also use its strong canine teeth to pierce the armor of reptiles. Tortoises and turtles are favorite prey of the jaguar, which is able to kill them by brute force.

The jaguar uses its canines to break apart the top of a tortoise shell to get the meat. To tackle the harder shell of a river turtle (below), it breaks into the sides and scoops out the meat with a paw. This taste for turtles, and for other water-living animals such as fish and caimans (relatives of alligators and crocodiles), may be what brings jaguars so often to the water s edge.

Louise H. Emmons

Comstock

Cheetahs

The name comes from a Hindu word *chita*, meaning "spotted one." The cheetah's light brown coat is covered with solid, round, black spots of various sizes. Its slender body, long and thin legs, and small skull make the cheetah different from other big cats.

One species

During the Pleistocene (2 million to 10,000 years ago) at least four species of cheetahs lived in North America, Africa, Europe, and Asia. Only one species has survived until today. Fossilized bones of this species have been dug up throughout Africa and Southwest Asia, as far as India, so it used to be widespread. Now the only places where the cheetah lives are savanna grasslands and dry areas with bushes in Africa south of the Sahara desert; and remote areas in Iran and northwest Afghanistan, where there may be only a couple of hundred.

Champion sprinters

In a "wildlife Olympics" competition, cheetahs would win gold medals in the 200 and 400 meter sprints. At top speed, a cheetah can run 68 miles per hour

▼ *One of the reasons cheetahs are probably the fastest animals on land is because of their "rotary gallop." This illustration shows how the cheetah sprints. Twice in the sequence all four feet are off the ground!*

▼ Bottom. *With an incredible burst of speed, a cheetah overtakes a fleeing Thomson's gazelle, a favorite prey of cheetahs in East Africa. The cheetah will kill the gazelle by biting down on its throat, until the gazelle suffocates. Cheetahs also hunt impalas, hares, and wildebeests.*

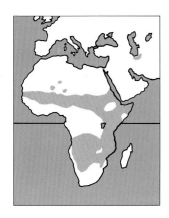

Royalty and other wealthy people in parts of Europe, the Middle East, and Asia used to train cheetahs to hunt for them. Other cheetahs were used in coursing, a sport that is similar to horse racing. Cheetahs breed poorly in captivity, so they were never domesticated—just captured and trained.

▼ Bottom. *Young cheetahs follow their mother across the East African plain. Cheetahs are slim, light, and elegant animals.*

(110 kilometers per hour), but only for a short distance. From a standing start, the cheetah can go from 0 to 68 in two seconds—so quick that we would see it only as a blur.

A sprinting cheetah moves in what is called a rotary gallop. As you can see in the series of pictures here, its hind limbs land first (on alternate sides), then it "floats" with all limbs outstretched off the ground. Next, the forelimbs land (on alternate sides), followed by a stage of crossed flight when all four feet are under its body.

All cats have bodies designed for speed. They walk and run with only their toes touching the ground (called a digitigrade stance), and they have flexible spines and high, mobile shoulders. In the cheetah's body these features are developed to the extreme. Compared to other cats, its feet and leg bones are straighter, its shoulders and limbs are longer, and its spine is longer and has larger muscles for flexing and stretching. The cheetah is also slimmer and lighter than other big cats, weighing only 88 to 143 pounds (40–65 kilograms). With these features it is the world's fastest cat.

Unusual social life

Cheetahs have an unusually flexible social system. Each female lives alone, except when cubs are with her. After the cubs leave their mother, they stay together for about six months, then the females separate and go off alone. Brothers stay together, in groups of two, three, or four, for the rest of their life, which lasts as long as eight years in the wild.

But people who study cheetahs have discovered two curious facts. The first is that almost half of male cheetahs live alone. The second fact is that, in many groups of males, some are brothers but others are unrelated. Older cubs who have lost their mother will sometimes latch onto an unrelated family or a group of males. These orphans survive by stealing meat from their "adopted" adults.

In Tanzania (East Africa), female cheetahs travel over huge areas—as big as 300 square miles (800 square kilometers)—because they follow Thomson's gazelles, which are migrating in search of fresh grass. The females' home ranges do overlap, of course, because one female could not possibly defend such a large area, but the females try to avoid each other.

Most males move over huge areas, too, but about a third of the males choose to defend territories, 15 square miles (40 square kilometers) in size. Important features of a territory are rocky outcrops or clumps of trees and bushes—the type of places that females choose for giving birth and raising their cubs. This means that territorial males are most likely to breed. Because male cheetahs fight fiercely to get a territory, most territories are owned by groups of males rather than by single males.

▲ *Separated from its mother and the rest of the herd, a confused baby gazelle is easy prey for a young cheetah. Young cheetahs often start their sprint too far away from prey, giving them time to escape.*

▼ *Cheetahs live in flat, open habitats where they can spot prey and predators in the distance. Cheetahs are active during the day, when the lions and hyenas that compete with them for prey are less likely to be out hunting.*

Did you know?

Life is very dangerous for baby cheetahs. In Tanzania's Serengeti National Park, nine out of ten cubs die before they are three months old. Exposure to rain, fire, and disease kills some cubs. Many others are eaten by lions, hyenas, jackals, and eagles.

▲ *Cheetah cubs begin to follow their mother on hunts at about six weeks of age. They stay with her until they are 14 to 18 months old.*

Pumas

The puma is the second-largest cat in the Western Hemisphere (after the jaguar), and the largest cat in most of North America.

What's in a name?

When European settlers arrived in North America, they named many animals after more familiar Old World creatures. Pumas were called American lions, after the African lions the females resemble. Some people called them panthers, a name often given to leopards, which pumas resemble in their adaptable nature. Other names are cougar, painter, and catamount (cat on the mountain). We use "puma," the name that the Incas of South America gave this cat, but other books may use mountain lion or cougar. And the pumas living in southern Florida are always called Florida panthers!

The adaptable American

Pumas are distributed over a bigger area than any other land mammal in the Americas. They are found from the Canadian Yukon in the north to the Straits of Magellan, at the tip of South America, in the south. Until a few hundred years ago, they also lived from the East Coast to the West of the United States and Canada, but now they are found only in the western regions—apart from the few that have managed to survive in southern Florida.

Like the wide-ranging leopard, the puma lives in many different habitats. It is at home in hot rain forests and cold evergreen forests,

▼ *This puma is using its scissor-like molar teeth to cut chunks of meat from a deer carcass. The puma has large pointed canine teeth to grab and kill prey, and small incisor teeth to get the last tiny bits of meat off a bone.*

Leonard Lee Rue III/Bruce Coleman Ltd

▲ *The puma and the lion are the only plain-coated big cats. The lion's coat is always tawny-brown, but a puma's coat may be reddish-brown, golden, blue-gray, or any shade in between. Puma kittens (and lion cubs) have a spotted coat until they are a few months old.*

Q. What is the Florida panther's greatest enemy?

A. Motor vehicles! In recent years, the number of pumas in southern Florida has fallen to fewer than 50. Many have been killed when crossing highways in Florida.

▼ *This puma feels threatened and is showing a defensive facial expression. Adult pumas have very few predators (other than people), but in the past, when grizzly bears and gray wolves were more numerous, they may have sometimes killed pumas.*

in high mountains and low canyons, in swamps and grasslands, and in sage brush and deciduous forest. The biggest pumas live in the far north and the far south; the largest individuals, the males, in these cold places weigh 227 pounds (103 kilograms). The smallest pumas, at 80 pounds (36 kilograms), live in tropical rain forests.

The search for food

Pumas in North America prey mostly on mule deer, white-tailed deer, and elk, but they also hunt smaller animals such as rabbits and ground squirrels. Pumas in the rain forests survive on small rodents, opossums, bats, and lizards. In the cool hills of Chile in western South America, pumas mostly kill guanacos (a smaller relative of camels) and hares.

Pumas hunt both during the day and at night. In Idaho, they hunt during the day in the summer, because that is when the ground squirrels come out of their underground burrows and are easy to capture. In the winter, they usually hunt for elk and deer in the evening and at night.

A puma travels widely over its home range to find large prey. It may stay with a large kill for up to 19 days, until all the meat is gone. (If a puma leaves a kill, coyotes, crows, or golden eagles will quickly find and eat it.) Then it moves 1 or 2 miles (2 to 3 kilometers) every day, zigzagging through thickets and across creeks, until it finds the next meal.

Scientists in Idaho have been able to study the puma's movements during the entire year, with radiotracking equipment, and some of the home ranges seem to be enormous. The range of one male that scientists radiotracked was 175 square miles (453 square kilometers). The largest home range of a radiotracked female was 144 square miles (373 square kilometers). In other parts of North and South America, a puma's home range may be larger or smaller, as long as it includes enough hoofed mammals and other animals so the cat can find sufficient food to survive. The home range must also have places where the puma can stalk its prey without being seen.

Did you know?

Pumas have much longer hind-legs than forelegs. This makes them good jumpers—just as the kangaroo's very large feet and hindlegs and tiny "arms" make it a good jumper. Pumas can leap across steep canyons and ravines in mountainous habitats.

Social life

A male puma defends his home range, or territory, from other males, but not from females. His home range usually overlaps with the home ranges of several adult females, who mate with him. The ranges of female pumas may partly overlap each other; but like most other solitary cats, the females try to avoid being in the same place at the same time.

Pumas do not fight about home ranges very often. Instead, they seem to "respect" the resident puma's land claims. A young puma will claim a home range only when a vacant area becomes available—when the resident puma dies or moves away. Pumas scent-mark and make "scrapes" (piles of brush or leaves that they urinate on) throughout their home ranges to tell other pumas that they are living there. Unlike lions, tigers, and leopards, pumas do not announce their presence with loud roars, although a female in estrus, who is ready to mate, may call very loudly to alert a distant male. The only time males and females come together is when they mate.

The female puma gives birth to two or three young, after a pregnancy of about three months. Until the kittens are about three months of age, their mother leaves them in the shelter of a thicket or in a cave while she hunts. The kittens begin to follow their mother on hunts and learn how to feed on kills; their mother stops nursing them at about the same time. Slowly the young learn to hunt for themselves.

By two years of age they are ready to strike out on their own. At this age, a puma is old enough to breed—but only if it can find a vacant home range. Until it does, it

▼ *Pumas go to water to drink but seldom go in it—as this mother seems to be telling her young.*

wanders among the ranges of others, but usually the young puma is not allowed by the adult pumas to stay in any one home range for very long.

Pumas on the rise

From the time that European settlers arrived in North America, they hunted and killed pumas. They feared these big cats, which sometimes preyed on their cattle, sheep, and horses. Pumas also hunt the same game—deer and elk—that people do. Many people believed that if the pumas were not wiped out, there would be less meat for themselves to eat.

Pumas quickly disappeared from eastern North America, except in southern Florida, where only a tiny population still survives. Southern Florida was once a remote wilderness, but the Florida panther is probably doomed by the development of its habitat for human uses.

The story is different in the western United States. For more than 100 years, hunters would shoot pumas on sight, and wildlife officials had permission to poison them. By 1960, pumas survived only in quite small pockets deep in mountainous wilderness areas. Then American attitudes toward big predators started to change, and many states rewrote their laws so that pumas were no longer treated as vermin. Hunting was regulated to limit the number of pumas killed each year, and poisoning programs were halted. As a result, the number of pumas is increasing in the West, and pumas are reappearing in more and more places where their ancestors lived. In Colorado and British Columbia, Canada, pumas have even been found living in the suburbs.

▲ *This raccoon is likely to escape. Pumas are agile climbers, but they usually hunt on the ground.*

Did you know?

The center of the ancient Inca civilization was the city of Cuzco (now in Peru), designed in the shape of a puma.

Many Native American people believed in gods with pumalike characteristics.

Alan and Sandy Carey

C.C. Lockwood/Animals Animals

Snow leopards

Snow leopards are the most mysterious of the big cats. They have a wonderful ability to blend into the rocky mountains and steep cliffs in Central Asia and are rarely seen by the people who live there.

The high life

No one knows how many snow leopards still roam the high mountains of Central Asia, an area called "the roof of the world." But a few scientists have ventured into the land of snow leopards to learn a little about their lives.

Snow leopards enjoy the high life. They are usually found at high altitudes above 9800 feet (3000 meters), and in summer they can climb up to 18,000 feet (5500 meters). For comparison, Mount Everest, the world's highest mountain, is 29,000 feet (8840 meters). This habitat is cold and dry, and the ground is often covered with snow and ice.

Snow leopards must be excellent climbers to live and hunt in the steep mountains. They have large forepaws, short front limbs, large chest muscles, and a long tail. The tail, 3 feet (1 meter) long, acts as a balance, like the bar carried by a tightrope walker. Snow leopards also climb and rest in trees, but they probably hunt on the ground.

Preying on wild sheep

A snow leopard weighs between 55 and 165 pounds (25–75 kilograms) and needs to kill 20 to 30 blue sheep each year to survive. Blue sheep, or bharal,

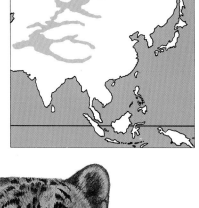

Vampire cats

Some people in Central Asia believe that snow leopards do not eat the meat of their prey but live by sucking their blood, like vampires. This idea probably came from villagers who scared the shy snow leopard away from its kill before it had a chance to begin eating. The only marks on the body of the prey were the small holes made by the snow leopard's sharp canine teeth.

Terry Whittaker/Frank Lane Picture Agency

▲ *Snow leopard cubs (two or three) are born in April, May, or June. They stay with their mother for about two years.*

◄ *Snow leopards are well adapted to their life in the mountains.*

▼ *A snow leopard rests in a conifer tree. In many places where snow leopards live, there is almost no vegetation.*

which is 5 to 15 square miles (12 to 39 square kilometers) in size. Snow leopards have been seen in small groups, but these are probably a mother and her almost-adult cubs. The home ranges of different snow leopards sometimes overlap, but no two animals use the same part of the range at the same time.

A rare cat

The snow leopard's habitat is huge—more than 1 million square miles (2.5 million square kilometers) in parts of Pakistan, Afghanistan, Tadzhikistan, Kirghizia, Kazakhstan, Mongolia, India, Nepal, Bhutan, Tibet and northeastern China. Over this area they have always been rare. But today they are disappearing from areas where they used to be seen regularly.

Hunting snow leopards is illegal in most countries, but many people still kill them for their beautiful spotted fur. You can easily understand that a very poor man from a mountain village might kill a snow leopard to earn money to feed his family. With the skin of one leopard, he can earn between 50 and 200 dollars, which is more than many of these villagers earn in an entire year. The people to blame are the traders and furriers, who get rich on his efforts, and the people who wear the skins. To make a full-length snow leopard coat takes 16 skins and sells for about $60,000, which is about 20 times as much as the poachers earned for their work.

weigh 88 to 132 pounds (40–60 kilograms), about the size of a female North American bighorn sheep. These sheep live in the same mountainous habitat as the snow leopard and are the snow leopard's most important prey.

However, the snow leopard isn't fussy. It also hunts small prey such as marmots and pheasants. It can even take huge yaks. When wild animals are scarce, snow leopards sometimes kill the domestic sheep and goats owned by the people of the mountains. Snow leopards usually hunt at dawn and dusk, or during the night.

Like other big cats, the snow leopard lives and hunts alone on a large home range,

Man-eaters

Why do big cats eat people? A better question might be: why don't they eat people more often? Big cats are larger, stronger, faster, and more agile than humans.

▲ *A wooden figure created for an 18th-century Indian ruler. The model is life-size, the man even groans and the tiger roars.*

Usually afraid of us

Cats eat primates such as monkeys and baboons; and human beings are primates, too. We know that our ancestors thousands of years ago were often attacked by big cats. But over the ages, big cats learned that preying on people—who are predators with great intelligence and dangerous weapons—simply wasn't worth it. Now they usually avoid people, treating humans with respect and even fear. In fact, when a lion attacks a man, it attacks him as if he were a predator to be feared, and not a item of prey like a zebra.

What, then, causes a tiger or lion to overcome its fear and attack people? Most often, it is simply hunger. Very old or disabled cats become man-eaters because they find people are much easier prey to capture than fleet-footed deer or antelope. If natural prey is difficult to catch, big cats (especially mothers with growing cubs to feed) will turn to people to supplement their diet. In Tanzania, for example, lions kill more people during the rainy season because that is when the tall grass makes it harder for lions to find natural prey.

Some become famous

Apart from these situations, most big cats do not go out of their way to hunt people but will kill and eat a person they come across by chance. There are famous man-eaters, however, who were healthy animals in their prime, and who lived among abundant natural prey animals, yet began killing people with a vengeance. No one knows why.

▼ *Excerpts from Colonel Patterson's diary.*

Keeping a balance

Because some conservation programs have been successful, the number of big cats in reserves and parks has increased. Now, fences and guns must be used to keep the cats and people away from each other.

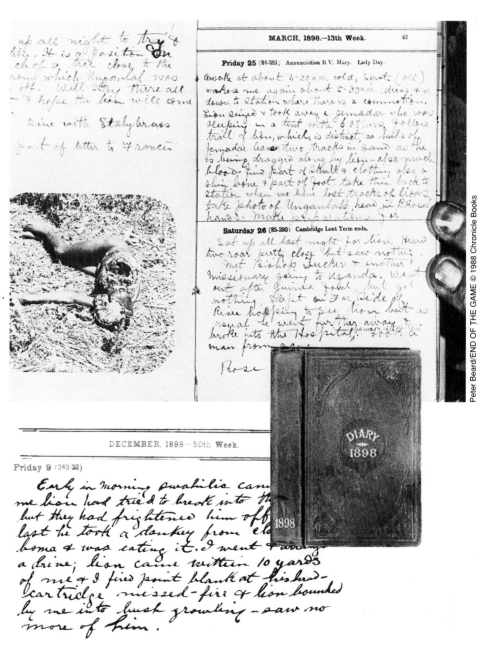

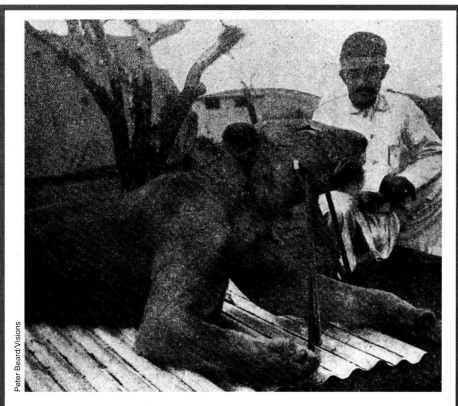

The Tsavo man-eaters

Colonel J. H. Patterson wrote a diary about his heroic efforts to kill the Tsavo man-eaters in Kenya. Patterson was an engineer in charge of building the Tsavo River bridge. He was not an experienced hunter, but he had to get rid of the lions that were holding up completion of the bridge.

Patterson shot the first Tsavo lion from a platform, and he found the second (pictured above) on foot, 18 days later. Patterson climbed a tree when the wounded lion charged him, but he finally killed it with his ninth bullet.

In northern India, one incredible tiger, known as the Champawat Tigress, killed 436 people—more than any other man-eater in history. She was the first man-eater killed by Jim Corbett, a hunter who became famous for tracking and killing man-eating tigers and leopards.

When people disrupt the natural balance between predator and prey, more tigers become man-eaters. It happens like this: People and their livestock move into tiger habitat, reducing the space available for tigers. With less space, some tigers are forced to live near a village, where wild prey are scarce because people like to eat the same animals as tigers do. So, these tigers turn to the village's domestic livestock for food. Their first human victim is usually a herdsman protecting his cows or goats. Then any person becomes fair game.

When lions become man-eaters

Lions become man-eaters less often than tigers, but when they do they are bolder and more aggressive in their pursuit of people. A man-eating lion often hunts at night and goes into villages looking for its victims.

This does make it easier for people to find and eliminate a man-eating lion than a man-eating tiger, so a lion usually has fewer victims. Still, one lion killed 84 people in Uganda during the 1920s. More recently, a group of lions killed 30 people in one year in Tanzania.

Leopards

Leopards rarely become man-eaters, but when one does, it hunts its human prey and escapes its human hunters with almost-diabolical cunning.

▲ *A colorful scroll showing man-eating tigers in the Sundarbans, India.*

◀ *Jim Corbett, the world-famous hunter of man-eating tigers, who shot the Champawat Tigress.*

53

For eight years, the man-eating leopard of Rudyaprayag terrorized the pilgrims along a route to Hindu shrines in northern India. This cat took 125 human lives. It survived various types of poison and rifle fire from two soldiers who ambushed it. It escaped from a box trap and from a leg-hold trap. Once it was sealed in a cave, but when the cave was opened it raced to freedom through a crowd of 500 people. Finally it was shot by hunter Jim Corbett after a month-long hunt.

Corbett also killed the man-eating Panwar leopard, which was less famous but more deadly, taking 400 victims.

Jaguars and other big cats

Although they are larger than leopards, jaguars are even less likely to prey on people. There are very few tales about jaguars deliberately hunting people for food, and no man-eating jaguar has become famous. Jaguars seem to kill people only when they feel threatened or when they mistake a person for another animal.

The same is true of pumas, although recently more puma attacks on people are being reported in the western United States,

where populations of both people and pumas are increasing.

Snow leopards and cheetahs have never been known to be man-eaters, although both species are capable of killing people.

▲ *The body of a man-killing tiger shot in 1915, in Hong Kong. It killed two policemen that were searching for it.*

▼ *Tigers have killed more people than any other big cat.*

Cunning opponents

"If the leopard were as big as the lion it would be ten times more dangerous."

John Taylor

Taylor's opinion of leopards was shared by Carl Akeley, also a famous big game hunter. He is pictured here with the carcass of a man-eating leopard, with which he has just had a close encounter!

Two-faced defense

The Sundarbans is an enormous area of mangrove forests at the delta of the Ganges and Brahmaputra rivers, in India and Bangladesh. Sundarbans means "beautiful forest," and it is home to more than 500 tigers. But the Sundarbans tigers have been notorious man-eaters.

No people live in the Sundarbans, but many go there to fish, collect honey, and cut wood. And many get eaten by tigers while doing so. Between 1975 and 1985, 612 people were killed by tigers, in most cases after a chance meeting in the forest. When it happens, the man-eating tigers are often hunted down and killed. To save both people and tigers, conservationists are trying new ways to prevent man-eating.

Scientists observed that tigers usually approach their prey from behind. So in 1987, Indian officials began to give brightly colored face masks to forest-users, who wear them on the back of the head. With two faces, a person has no behind, and the tigers are fooled into thinking a person is watching them. It seems to work: none of the thousands of people who have worn the mask in the forest have been attacked, even though tigers have been seen following them.

Another approach is to teach tigers to fear people. Life-sized mannequins wired to a car battery are left in the forest for tigers to find. If a tiger attacks, it gets a nasty shock—and may think twice about attacking the next person it sees.

▲ One way to repel tigers is to electrify mannequins. When a tiger attacks the model it gets a nasty shock. Scientists hope that this will teach the tiger to avoid people.

▶ Villagers working in the Sundarbans wear face masks on the backs of their heads to prevent tiger attacks. Tigers generally attack from behind, but with the face masks the villagers don't have a "behind."

Raghu Rai/Magnum

Conservation of big cats

All the big cats are endangered or threatened in all or parts of their range. Several factors are causing the decline of big cats all over the world. How is each species faring?

Tigers number about 5000 individuals in the wild. They are the most endangered of the big cats.

Lions are still numerous in Africa, where about 200,000 live. Only a few hundred Asian lions survive in India.

Leopards exist in quite good numbers throughout their range, but everywhere they are declining.

Jaguar numbers are also declining. Only about 1000 live in the whole of Mexico and Central America, and jaguars may be extinct in some parts of South America.

Snow leopards At most about 5000 snow leopards live in Central Asia.

Cheetahs The world population of the cheetah is about 14,000 animals, half the number that existed 15 years ago.

Pumas are increasing in western North America, but the Florida panthers are probably doomed to extinction. The puma's status in Central and South America is uncertain but probably mirrors the jaguar's.

The skin trade

The spotted big cats have been greatly reduced in numbers during this century, as modern guns have made the cats easy to kill. The reason is the enormous demand for fur coats made of beautiful skins.

In 1975, the trade in spotted cat fur was controlled for the first time, when representatives of 100 countries signed the Convention of International Trade in Endangered Species (CITES). International trade in skins and other parts of tigers, cheetahs, snow leopards, leopards, and jaguars is now illegal; and most countries either ban or regulate the hunting of big cats.

Yet spotted fur still gets a high price on the black market, so many cats are killed by poachers. Many of their body parts are still used in traditional Asian medicines.

Habitat loss

There is less and less wilderness for big cats. All of the big cats need big areas to find enough prey to survive. In some places they depend on prey that people like to hunt; and big cats sometimes prey on domestic livestock. People and big cats are now competing for the same resources—land and food—and the cats are losing the competition.

▲ *Villagers use sharpened bamboo spears topped with poison to kill snow leopards that prey on their livestock.*

▶ *Although it lives in remote areas, the snow leopard is hunted for its skin.*

◀ *Some traditional people wear capes made of leopard fur during their cultural and religious ceremonies. These cultural traditions may die out as leopards become rare, although they have little effect on big cat numbers.*

Pet predators

Many people love cats. Around the world, there are about 100 million domestic cats kept as pets. But some people prefer their cats to be bigger. In Italy, for instance, about 3000 lions, tigers, and leopards are kept as pets. Unfortunately the existence of these big cats does not help conservation efforts because they are not available for breeding with wild populations or others in zoos.

A species under threat

Until recently, large regions in the snow leopard's territory were virtually uninhabited by people. Now, local people and their livestock have moved into many areas. This has caused a depletion of the snow leopard's natural prey, and as a result, the snow leopard has turned to preying on domestic animals. People respond by killing snow leopards. This, in addition to the illegal fur trade, is why snow leopards are declining in numbers.

The future of big cats

Big cats can survive if people let them. Conservationists believe that people must do five things to save big cats.

1. Build public support
People in towns and cities can help by persuading their political leaders that saving the big cats is important. They can also help by contributing time or funds to conservation groups working around the world to save big cats.

The usually poor rural people who live among big cats must support their conservation, too. This means that governments and conservationists must find solutions to the problems of living with big cats, such as loss of livestock and human lives. Rural people should benefit from saving big cats. For example, many tourists travel to national parks around the world for a chance to see big cats; and when rural people can make money from these tourists, they are more likely to want to save the cats.

2. Conserve the habitats of big cats
National parks and reserves that protect predators and their prey are important to the survival of big cats. More parks need to be created, and well protected. They need to be large enough to support at least 250 individual cats of each species living in the area. "Corridors" of habitat should connect parks and reserves so that cats can move between them to breed.

3. Breed big cats in zoos, to support their conservation in the wild
Zoos educate people about big cats. The staff at zoos study the cats and learn about their breeding biology and management; this helps biologists to manage big cats in the wild. Zoo breeding programs will help to ensure that, if a species becomes extinct in the wild, there are big cats of the same species that can be set free in the future.

4. Learn more about big cats in the wild
If people and big cats are to coexist, we must know more about how cats live, how human activities affect them, and how they interact with other wildlife in their habitat. This information will help wildlife managers to deal with problems, such as inbreeding, insufficient prey, and big cats killing domestic livestock and people. More scientists are needed to acquire this information, and they need funds to support their research.

5. Control the international trade in skins and other body parts
Governments must do a better job enforcing the laws against poaching and trading in fur and other body parts of big cats.

It is hard to imagine a world without big cats, but there is no good reason why we have to. If people take action to save them, they will survive.

Betty Press/Animals Animals

▲ *Cheetahs live in a vast wilderness area within Kenya's Masai Mara Reserve and Tanzania's Serengeti National Park in East Africa.*

Did you know?

People in Kenya have a real interest in saving their big cats. Tourists spend a lot of money when they come to see the wildlife—each year it equals about $515,000 for every adult male lion living in Kenya's Amboseli National Park.

▶ *Scientists study tigers from the backs of elephants in Nepal. What they have learned in the past 20 years has helped to save Nepal's tigers and tiger habitat.*

◀ *Lion cubs in Kora Game Reserve, Kenya.*

Cats in zoos

As the area of wilderness for big cats shrinks, it is becoming more and more important to save them in zoos. Zoos have always exhibited big cats. They give city people a chance to marvel at these magnificent predators, far from the big cats' natural habitat.

Breeding programs

Today, zoos give the highest priority to breeding big cats, so that future generations of people will have big cats to marvel at. Big cats raised in zoos may someday be returned to natural habitats where their wild cousins have become extinct.

Most big cats living in zoos were born in zoos, not taken from the wild. Zoo managers study big cats, and use information from studies of big cats in the wild, so that they can make the animals' diet, habitat, and social groupings as natural as possible. This gives the cats a better chance to breed successfully.

How zoos help each other

Zoo managers are careful matchmakers and don't allow close relatives to mate. They know that inbreeding (mating between close relatives) leads to a high rate of infant deaths and other problems in reproduction. To prevent inbreeding they make sure that the male and female in a breeding pair are as distantly related as possible. Cats are often moved from zoo to zoo so the best pairs can get together.

In North America, most zoos cooperate in Species Survival Plans (SSPs) for big cats, which are organized by the American Association of Zoological Parks and Aquariums. Siberian and Sumatran tigers,

◀ Lions, tigers, and leopards have been popular with zoo visitors for a long time.

Mary Evans Picture Library

Hulton-Deutsch

Did you know?

More than 160 Sumatran tigers live in zoos around the world, but only about 500 exist in the wild. Zoo biologists hope that breeding programs for tigers in captivity will ensure that Sumatran tigers do not become extinct like the Bali, Javan, and Caspian tigers.

◀ The zoo in Regent's Park, London, in about 1900. Modern zoos no longer exhibit big cats in such bare and dismal cages.

animals, and when to move and breed them. Especially for endangered species such as the Siberian tiger, this keeps the zoo population growing and helps to maintain a high level of genetic diversity. (Inbreeding reduces genetic diversity.) The master plans also help conservation efforts to save big cats in the wild. Zoos in Europe, Australia, and Japan have similar programs for endangered big cats.

Big cats living in small populations—isolated in national parks and other wildlife reserves—may soon have to be managed to prevent inbreeding and possible extinction in the wild. If so, the knowledge about how to save big cats in zoos will help people to save them in the wild.

snow leopards, cheetahs, and Asian lions are all SSP species. Scientists from the zoos have worked together to write a master plan for each species, outlining the best pairings of

Q. What is genetic diversity?

A. Genetic diversity is the amount of variation in the genes of all members of a species. This variation is what causes individual differences. In the long term, it allows animals to adapt to changing conditions in the environment. If there is no variation, the animals may die when their environment suddenly becomes different. A whole species may become extinct. If the animals have the ability to adapt to change, they will live. If not, they will die.

Scientists think that when a population in the wild has at least 250 adult cats, they can maintain genetic diversity.

Robbi Newman/The Image Bank

▶ *These pumas are mating in a zoo, but it looks like their natural habitat. In modern zoos, exhibits like this help to teach visitors about big cats and their threatened habitats.*

Big cats and human culture

The magnificent big cats inspired people of the Ice Age, 15,000 years ago, to paint pictures of lions on the walls of caves. Since then, in cultures around the world, big cats have appeared in myths and legends, as gods and symbols.

Western culture

Lions were the most familiar of the big cats to Europeans. They appear in Ice Age cave paintings and, thousands of years later, on ancient Greek coins. In the art of medieval Europe, lions symbolized Jesus Christ. They also symbolized strength and power, so when the English king, Richard, was nicknamed "the Lionhearted," the phrase may have had the double meaning of a powerful *and* religious man.

The lion is the national symbol of the Netherlands, and it appears on many European flags and coats of arms. Lions continue to represent power—as mascots for sports teams and in commercial advertising. You may have noticed that sculptures of lions, in pairs, guard the entrance to castles, churches, and public buildings such as libraries and museums.

Tigers are Asian animals, of course, and they appeared later than lions in the art and culture of Europe. But once these animals were known, they too inspired artists and writers. Tigers became another symbol of strength and power, often combined with stealth, in contrast to the bold image of lions.

▲ *In ancient Rome the emperor Nero persecuted Christians by feeding them to the lions. This scene was drawn by a French artist in about 1887 for a poster to advertise a circus.*

The Granger Collection, New York

The artists' view

In Europe during the Middle Ages, until about A.D. 1300, lions were drawn in a

▼ Tropical Story with a Tiger, *by Henri Rousseau, 1891.*

The drama of tigers

William Shakespeare often used tiger images in his plays. Here, Romeo speaks of his fierce love for Juliet, which he compares to the hunger of a tiger:

> The time and my intent are savage-wild,
> More fierce and more inexorable far
> Than empty tigers or the roaring sea.

And Henry V encourages his weary soldiers to act like tigers at the battle of Agincourt:

> But when the blast of war blows in our ears,
> Then imitate the action of the tiger;
> Stiffen the sinews, summon up the blood,
> Disguise fair nature with hard-favor'd rage;
> Then lend the eye a terrible aspect.

stylized way. As symbols of Christ or power, a lion image did not need to be accurate; it simply had to be recognized. Later, during the Renaissance, people became more interested in the natural world, and lions were brought to Europe for people to see and marvel at. Artists were able to see them close up, and their images of lions became more realistic. But lions were often painted as ferocious beasts which had been tamed by the piety of gentle saints.

Starting in the 19th century, artists began to paint realistic lions and tigers in a wilderness background, although sometimes their wild environment was rather fanciful.

These artists admired the big cats for their beauty, speed, and strength, and for their very wildness. Today, many wildlife artists try to portray realistic big cats in realistic environments, inspiring us to save these magnificent predators.

Asian art and culture

In many Asian cultures, tigers were a symbol of strength and royal power. Only noblemen could hunt them, and tigers were used as executioners in Asian courts.

In the Hindu religion, the god Shiva rides a tiger and wears a tiger skin for his role as destroyer. In the Buddhist religion, followers of Buddha ride tigers to show their supernatural ability to overcome evil. Many forest people in India treated tigers like gods and built temples and shrines for tiger worship. Among the followers of Islam in Sumatra, tigers are believed to punish sinners for Allah.

There are many Asian legends about "were-tigers"—people who can turn themselves into tigers. In some of these legends, groups of were-tigers were said to live like humans in villages. Similar legends of were-lions and were-leopards existed in Africa; and were-jaguars were a feature of South American cultures.

Tigers in Chinese art

Images of tigers were used more than 3000 years ago in the art of China's Shang dynasty, from 1700 to 1050 B.C. The Shang people believed that tigers were powerful messengers between the human world and the spirit world. In the next dynasty, the Zhou, from 1050 to 221 B.C., tiger sculptures were more realistic, with deadly fangs, long claws, and swelling muscular shoulders. These artists had clearly seen tigers alive and were in awe of their lethal power.

Later artists focused on tigers as powerful and also beneficial to people. Images of

Did you know?

Tigers once lived throughout China. There, the tiger was considered to be the king of the beasts, just like lions in Western cultures. When painting the stripes on a tiger's head, Chinese artists often wrote the Chinese character for "king."

▲ *The tiger and the dragon in this picture represent the two great forces of nature—*yin *(the tiger) and* yang *(the dragon), which are part of Taoist philosophy.*

Jenny Mills

The Granger Collection, New York

tigers were placed on tombs to keep evil spirits away and protect the souls of the dead. Paintings of tigers asleep among Buddhist monks were meant to symbolize the religion's power to tame the wilder forces of nature.

In the 20th century, Chinese artists used the tiger as a national symbol. When Japan threatened to take over China, a painting of a roaring tiger showed the anger and fighting spirit of the Chinese people.

Lions in Chinese art

Lions are not native to China, and many artists imagined them as fantastic creatures with wings and other unrealistic features. The first record of a live lion in China is from the year 87 B.C., when a Central Asian prince, who wanted to marry a Chinese princess, sent one in exchange for her. For a while the people of ancient Rome traded lions for Chinese silk.

After the Buddhist religion was introduced to China (from India), Chinese artists showed Buddha seated on a throne supported by a pair of lions. Temples were guarded by a pair of stone lions, and gradually lions became the protectors of other buildings such as palaces, government offices, and even private gardens. They

weren't as fanciful as the winged lions of earlier Chinese dynasties, but lions at palaces built between 1368 and 1911 were still unrealistic—even the females were given a full mane. And some artists depicted a cub under its mother's paw, believing that lions received milk from their mother's paw.

Tovy Adina/Explorer

▲ *This gilded bronze lion is one of a pair that protects the Gate of Supreme Harmony, in the Forbidden City where the emperors lived in Beijing, China.*

▼ *This beautiful glazed brick panel of a lion dates back to ancient Babylon, where lions were symbols of royal power.*

Glossary

CANINE TEETH   The teeth between the front incisor teeth and the side molars. Long, sharp canine teeth are a feature of all cats.

CARNIVORA   A large scientific grouping, or order, of mammals, most of which are meat-eaters. Cats belong to the order Carnivora. So do dogs and bears.

CARNIVORE   Any animal that eats meat or flesh. Many animals (including people) are carnivores but do not belong to the order Carnivora.

CONSERVATION   The attempt to maintain the earth's natural resources, including wildlife, for future generations.

DIGITIGRADE STANCE   Walking on the toes, so that the heels do not touch the ground. The foot bones of cats are modified so that only their toes touch the ground. Human stance, walking with the entire foot on the ground, is called plantigrade.

ESTRUS   The period when a female mammal is ready to mate with a male to produce young.

EXTINCT   No longer living. When the last living member of a species dies, the species becomes extinct.

FAMILY   A scientific grouping of several species with similar features. Cats belong to the family Felidae.

GENETIC DIVERSITY   The amount of variation that exists in the genes of all the individual members of a species.

GENUS   A scientific grouping of species that are more closely related to each other than to any other species.

HABITAT   The place where an animal lives in the wild, such as a forest or a grassland. An animal's habitat provides food, water, shelter, and the right environment for the animal's survival.

HOME RANGE   The area that an animal travels over, during the course of a year, to find food and shelter, to find mates, and to raise young.

INBREEDING   Breeding between close relatives. Inbreeding often results in the death of many infants, greater susceptibility to disease, and reproductive problems.

PLEISTOCENE   The period between 2 million and 10,000 years ago, often called the Ice Age. Many very large animals became extinct at the end of the Pleistocene.

POACHING   Hunting wild animals illegally.

PREDATOR   An animal that hunts, kills, and eats other animals to survive.

PREY   Animals that are hunted, killed, and eaten by other animals called predators.

PRIDE   A group of lions.

PRIMATES   Monkeys, apes, and people.

SCAVENGER   An animal that survives by eating meat killed by other predators.

SPECIES	A group of animals with very similar features. Individual members of a species are able to breed and produce live young that are fertile (able to breed when they themselves become adults); they do not breed with members of other species. The species is the basic unit in scientific classification of plants and animals.
SUBSPECIES	Members of a species that consistently differ in certain features from other members of the species—although not enough so that individuals can no longer breed and produce live, fertile young. Subspecies are usually separated from each other by barriers such as seas or high mountains.
TERRITORY	An area that an animal (or group of animals) lives in, and which it defends from other members of its species, especially those of the same sex. An animal's home range is called a territory if the animal does not allow others of the same sex to enter it.

List of scientific names

Common name	Scientific name
cheetah	*Acinonyx jubatus*
puma	*Felis concolor*
jaguar	*Panthera onca*
leopard	*Panthera pardus*
lion	*Panthera leo*
snow leopard	*Panthera uncia*
tiger	*Panthera tigris*

Each of the big cats in this book has a common name and a scientific name. Most of us call the various species by their common names: "lion" or "tiger" or "leopard." These are the names used by most English-speaking people, so you can be pretty sure that when you say "tiger" people know you are talking about the striped cat from Asia. But different people around the world have different common names for all the big cats. And even among English-speakers, pumas are also known as cougars, panthers, and mountain lions, and leopards are sometimes called panthers.

Scientists avoid any confusion created by multiple names for the same animal, by giving a two-word scientific name to each species. This system was invented by Carl von Linne (also known as Linneaus) in the 1700s. The first word is the genus (or group) the animal belongs to. *Panthera*, for instance, is the genus name of five species of big cats. The second word is the species name. For instance, *leo* is the species name for lions. Scientists always use two words to name a species, thus *Panthera leo* is the scientific name for lions. The scientific names are usually from Latin and Greek words.

When two or more species belong to the same genus, it means that they are quite closely related. The five big cats in the genus *Panthera* are more closely related to each other than they are to cheetahs or pumas.

Cheetahs are the only cats in the genus *Acinonyx*; and scientists are not sure how cheetahs are related to the other big cats. Pumas are now in the genus *Felis*, which also includes most small cats and domestic cats. If new studies of the puma's genetics prove that pumas are closer to the other big cats, scientists will change the genus name.

Index